The Mystical Life

Of Zenith Candlebaum

Sebastian Chalela Morris

Made with ❤ on the BookLeaf Publishing Platform

www.bookleafpub.in

www.bookleafpub.com

Dedication

To my wife Andy, forever the light of love. Without you, my song would be a quarter note, at best.

To my niece, nephews, and sister; forever the light of hope.

To my parents, their siblings, my ancestors, and my clan; forever the light of wisdom and companionship.

Preface

The following poems weave a single story; therefore, it is suggested that the first reading be done in the order they are presented. Subsequent readings should be done by skipping around and feeling the illusory need for order.

Or just ignore this preface; in the end, it's all an ever-changing game.

Acknowledgements

I want to express my deepest gratitude to my wife for her unwavering support, patience, and love; all key components for the creation of this work.

To the Chalela family: thank you for Intellect and Discipline.

To the Morris family: thank you for Art and Poetry.

To the Mantilla family: thank you for Music and Languages.

To the Castellanos family: thank you for Magic.

Epilogue

Zenith went back to the fields
where he had once gazed down at the sky
hoping for a sign or a shimmer,
a clue of the time he had been
there,
a someone there,
whose breath had been filled with a promise:
daring, adventure, romance.

Maybe time had eddied and pooled then
allowing greatness a moment
to stir up his bones
and swell huge his heart.

Maybe then he had cherished another,
a dream that felt warm to the touch,
lips that spoke only in whispers
Causing ripples across space and time.

All of it faded unreal now.
A thick haze remained beclouding his thoughts.
A jigsaw in pieces scattered over dirt,
his broken skin burrowed with ditches of yearning.

How he wished a past, any past, would revive!
His every cell aching to glimpse hues of color,
a light in the monochromes dancing for his eyes.

Invention without a conclusion
is all that he seems to know now.
True,
time had never stopped chipping away
at the stick figures he tried to preserve.
The wish to freeze-frame memory;
the insurmountable task of a Corinthian king.

Too tired, too drowned, too far gone.
The fields witness blossoming his utmost goodbye.
Off into the starless, black sky,
Thrust into the mist to cut through to the start.

First Days

Big Momma's chest heaves up and down
in agitation
Her immense breasts like rolling hills
make up my pillow
My tiny feet knead cat-Ike strokes
around her belly
The fuzzy end down by her legs
a secret window

Her eyes reflect comets and stars
all constellations
Her lips hide pearls shiny like droplets
from the sea
My chubby hands lost in her hair
pinch coiling twisters
as I discover feelings, ideas,
sensation

She inhales and clouds swell up with
anticipation
A million seeds prepare to bloom
face to the sky
She exhales changing earthquakes
into vegetation

She spurs the sun and moon around
breeding a tempo

All life explodes with song and dance
into existence
She smiles and I jump up and down
in celebration
With just one kiss she lets me know
the revelation
Knowing the game goes round and round
She grants me freedom

I love Big Momma's roots, her ground,
forests and valleys
Her open heart and love unbound
that flow eternal
Thank you Big Momma, now I'm off
to grow, discover
Honey and mud, cotton and stone
throughout your kingdom

Triumph

Zenith wiggled his restless toes and dug them one inch
deep into the sand.
He spread out his pudgy arms and flashed a smile at the
horizon.
The ocean played along by shrinking, growing, then
crashing a wave right at his feet.
A lord! Master of all, owner of nothing.

He swam with fish, and water turned his skin into
iridescent scales.
He flew with birds, and feathery colors sprouted from his
back.
He sang with frogs and roared with lions. He marched
with ants and blinked with stars.
A river! A flow bathing it all along his path.

He knew he was the worm wriggling through soil,
the leaves crowning the tree,
the bright petals of flowers.

To one and all he felt the deep connection; the single
pumping heart, the cell, the jiggling atoms.

To one and all he reached out with his radiance; tingling,

playful fingers working to amplify joy.

With one and all this love he wished to share.

Not bound by time.
Not chained by space.
He let the twirling clouds whisk him away.

The Bureau Of Dictation

The place was filled with derelict construction,
and monuments of stone crumbled by time.
It was known as the Bureau of Dictation,
where those who thought were wise came to prescribe.

The self-proclaimed wisemen pointed fingers and then
spoke,
spitting relentless questions meant to chisel widened
states
into simplified shapes suiting their purpose.

Asked about who he was,
Zenith had to bring forth a being smaller than himself.

Asked about what he did,
his potential was compressed, crushing the prospects for
his doing.

Asked about where he came from,
gravity stuck him to the ground and bound him to a
single place.

Asked about when he was born,
his free spirit shackled by dread now weighed him down,

enslaved by time.

Asked about why he was there,
he was tethered to a single, dictatorial purpose.

The entrapment had begun.

Now doubt had swapped his wings for chains.

The Ibigi

"See me!"
Demanded the Ibigi in a shrill voice.
"Everything I want is the only thing of relevance.
I am the most important Ibigi in this whole world.
Me, me, me!
I like things how I like them and that's how you need to
make them.
Only if I feel happy, then may you be happy too."

"Now take my misery!"
Screeched the Ibigi.
"You! Soak up all my tears, absorb all of my poison.
Forget about all others, if they don't play my symphony.
It matters not to me whether you rot or simply break.
Pile up all of your efforts to lighten up my day.
Mine, mine, mine!"

Zenith turned his back and started to walk away.

"No! Please don't go."
Pleaded the Ibigi.
"Don't you dare take another step!
I promise I will love you if your attention is on me.
But if your focus wavers,

Curse you!
You'll stay a simple flea."

"It's easy,
can't you see?
Only I matter,
me, me, me..."
Quacked on the Ibigi.

Zenith still heard it in the distance, as he ran,
ran, ran to flee.

Terror

The road led down into a dark ravine
where thorny vines crisscrossed
forming ominous patterns.
A wailing could be heard
behind the rotting brambles.

The desperate cries slowly drew Zenith in.
A man lay on the moss,
his chest looked dry and flattened,
lice crawled over his beard,
his words a croaky ramble.

"Look upon me you who are still pristine!
See your future reflected
on broken limbs, decaying skin.
See how my nails are falling,
and all my liquids pour
out of these orifices
now beyond my control.

The codes that build your system
have flaws in their defense,
so outside agents will infect,
attack, and vanquish them.

And even if you somehow manage
to make your physique strong
the failure will come from within
in blood, a wrecking throng.

Not you, not I, not them,
will outrun pain, disease,
and worse, there's nothing at the end
to hear your anguished pleas."

For the first time, Zenith felt weak,
unraveling, he cried.
He felt something in his heart tweak
and no matter how hard he tried,
he could not stop asking himself
if to this fate he was so tied.

Defiling Whispers

Perception has become an iteration,
no longer a totality.
I filter all impressions,
broken pieces of data
that hardly build a whole.
I don't know what is broken.
Did I do something wrong?
Now everything's in disarray,
I don't know where to go.

"Look here, look at this shiny pearl,
it's everything you need.
Maybe gold is what you require
to purchase on every whim.
Now salivate over that body.
Obsess with thoughts of fame and praise."

Like hooks the words pierced through his skin,
and kept on digging deeper, deep within.

"Take one thing, grab it all!
You know you want to own it.
Objectify all that you see,
keep it and save it,

stash it, hoard it.
Fill every longing.
Clog every hole.
Plug every lack.
Go get it all, all, all!

You will not feel confused again,
you'll disappear in isolation.
Make things your inert company,
materialism your salvation;
sing loud my praise: Desire! Amen!

And if you're feeling sad or sore,
feel like you are about to crack,
GET MORE!"

To Become A Memory

Zenith had been following the dog
over dirt roads,
and barren fields
under a scorching sun.

Its course seemed to be anything but certain,
led only by its nose,
tail tucked between its legs.

Not once did it seek shelter under roofs,
nor did it stop to pee on tree or shrub.

Panting it trotted on,
its lolling tongue gliding close to the ground,
ignoring puddles and fountains of water.

It crawled under a fern into the woods.
It lay under an elder.
It stretched stiff all its legs,
and forever shut its eyes.

Zenith gently petted the dog's spirit,
and learned its name in life...

He had lived with four humans.
They'd fed him, bathed him, loved him.
Sometimes they had ignored his needs,
his pleas to go outside,
and beat him when his innards stained the floor;
Boom! Boom!

Sometimes they had felt angry, misunderstood or sad,
and beat him once again;
Boom! Boom!

His carcass dry, and now eaten by worms,
diluting to become part of the forest,
reflection of the end to every story.

His loyalty, his servitude: his worth;
the stoic song heard by heavenly chorus,
required to become a memory.

The Other

I walked between the ferns and came into the jungle.
The silence pierced my ears,
the pungent smell, my nostrils.
The Other moved about dodging the light,
jumping from gloom to shadow,
treading with care and luring me to follow.

"Hello, goodbye; from now I'll be your friend.
I will protect your secrets.
I will cover with balsam all your pain."

Of these things, I knew nothing.
I did not understand.

The stormy night fell heavy; it jabbed its raven talons in
my shoulder,
and once it closed its wings
The load started to crush me.
Crush me.
Crush me.

"I'll help you carry the unwanted weight.
I'll give you claws to rip through desolation.
But you must keep me hidden,

keep me behind closed doors,
shield me from prying eyes,
and give me full control
when the monsters outside
threaten your fragility."

The Other can be scary.
The Other can be mean.
But I see the world breaking;
I'd rather stay within.

Veiled Rigging

Below him sat a crowd
looking upon a stage
on which musicians played
a dire, crushing tune.

The strings wailed and squealed high
like animals at slaughter.
The drummer banged, bonged, crashed
as if calling to war.

No harmony, no tempo,
only shrill, blasting screeches,
and the filth pouring from the singer's mouth
could have drowned sky, sea, and beaches.

Yet still, the crowd clapped on
excited beyond measure.
Their bulging eyes protruding from their heads,
their ears bleeding, their skin outstretched,
and still, they danced and howled amazed.

"The masses are bound to copy each other,
swayed to act like mindless drones.
They'll sacrifice will, and hand in their bones

to follow the trends dictated by another.

Blunted by the mundane, they crave a distraction.
They binge on excitement to feel they're alive.
They eat what they're fed without asking questions.
And if they're disturbed, even with good intentions,
their anger burns hot, they react like a hive.

One's easily caught in the wake of their need;
it is natural to want to belong.
But acting without thought is a terrible wrong,
it's fertilizer for ignorance, that murderous weed!"

The Madman On The Mountain

"I am the only one able to talk to God",
said the megalomaniac climbing atop the mountain.
"This power was granted to me by the heavenly host.
Being born nobler than most,
my mandate must be followed, my word spread far
abroad".

"Mine is the prerogative to understand the stars",
He said over the crowd that pointed at him, shouting.
"And so, I know what will befall you all that choose to
stray.
Now is the time to pray,
before demonic armies ravage us all with their wars".

"Refrain from all enjoyment, we are here to endure pain".
As Zenith looked around amazed, he saw nods of
agreement.
"You're all born tainted, filthy, tarnished by generations
past
so, if you want to last,
do as I say to cleanse your sin; we'll see paradise again".

"Renounce worldly possessions, bring them forth for me

to keep".

The crowd had fallen to their knees and threw at him
their payment.

"Be humble, obey my reign and I'll lead you to the plot
where crops grow without rot;
there you'll become pristine and worthy, like all
compliant sheep".

"I know this to be true; it's written in this book of law".
Since people didn't do much reading, they were ripe for
the taking.
"If you abide, and work, and toil, thinking only of Him,
like tokens, you'll redeem
every single salty drop that has perspired from your
brow".

"And women, be obedient and support your husband's
labor".
Zenith's fury was rising, he could not stop his hands
shaking.
"Raise children, keep the homestead, do at night your
wifely duty;
in submissiveness there's beauty.
Do this and more, holding your tongues, and you'll be in
God's favor".

"How can any of you believe this discourse!" Zenith

shouted.

The crowd turned around to face him

wanting to rip him limb from limb;

but the Other had readied escape and with him Zenith

bolted.

Defeat

I must have stepped into some misconfiguration.
Maybe I made a wrong turn that disturbed the
tessellation.
The interconnected mosaic that promised to be my life
has undergone extreme degeneration.

I no longer see light in the creations I encounter.
The bliss that I imagined seems to be missing a rafter.
Pain has become the foremost, and most prevalent
sensation.
Unstable truth has turned me into a doubter.

Now I despise my station,
and I can feel my stomach's churning fire.
The situation's dire.
I curse this exploration that leads only to frustration.

I wish my hands were claws
to rip apart the lies that made me dream.
The slate must be wiped clean,
and no myopic beings shall be allowed to create laws.

This world should be destroyed.
Cauterize this infection!

We are all drowning, all enslaved
by instilled trepidation.

Hourglass Haven

Zenith decided to lie down and curled into a ball.
Feeling drained, stepped on, squashed, diminished,
he hoped that snow would fall
and cover him 'til death's embrace
or 'til the world was finished.

The memory of his origin seemed lost; an absurd thought
fit only for fools and the obtuse,
broken ideas wrought
from wishing to escape the race
that all are meant to lose.

But existence knows when to play the ace under its
sleeve;
and she came singing over the hill
dressed in mysterious eve,
transforming the light of the place,
reigniting Zenith's will.

He stood and rubbed his eyes to confirm he was not
dreaming.
The woman smiled, she waved, became
the reason to keep living.
She wandered on; Zenith gave chase

begging her for her name.

"Most think me love, but I know that I'm more
infatuation.
Explaining it won't help, so come,
we'll live out your obsession.
The years will fly, you'll be amazed,
but soon I'll have my fill,
and so will you, pairs always do; it's etched in human
nature.
I predict that we'll build together,
and hardships we'll endure.
Suddenly we'll be wishing days
would not drag on forever.
You will know you have tasted love before I break your
heart.
So sear that feeling in your chest;
love is a complex art,
the key to burst free form this maze,
its purest form, the final quest."

Song For Kitty Cat

By Zenith Candlebaum

Across the valley, the mountain's lit with fire
The ocean's sirens fill my heart with song
Breath from your lips kissing away all my fears
Rocking me to my core
Devouring me whole

Kitty cat purring in my ear
Your words are the heaven I want to hear
Sweet girl, your love is a wild thing
I crave the trouble you get me in

My hands are aching to surf on your skin
I'm blinded by the lightning from your heart
You're the ocean, I'm free diving, sinking in
Flowing through the magical
Extension of our soul

Kitty cat, gazing at your eyes
My brain dissolves into butterflies
I am your fool, I'll be with you
Until I'm out of lives and the world is through

I had never seen grace like yours
Able to bring a spark to the dead
My pain cocoon has now been shed
Refined, I'm no longer a boor
The dissonance crowding my head
By your deliverance has fled
Your gospel is the one to spread
Of you, I will always want more.

Synergetic Ascent

"Do you hear the dark forest deep inside?
The wild geography howling beyond
the programs that have chained you to
an illusion that won't let you feel alive?

Do you feel the secrets swirling on the lake?
Thundering bolts of lightning, pushing to the surface
where your mask is fading
and your skin is waiting for the rain?

I am the untamed just outside your door,
the pull that magnetizes you,
bringing you to the shore
where sensuous gestures
lift us to the spheres
beyond all pain.

Let us navigate the incorporeal planes
resulting from our intertwining flesh
galloping without reins.
We'll birth a galaxy of choirs,
reach heaven with our spires,
and become rain.

Give into me, hold nothing back,
forget your history, your name;
with open arms take my attack.
I will melt your ego's persistence,
shake the foundations of existence,
pulverize time!"

Saint

By Zenith Candlebaum

A saint is one who feels herself
after shedding her costume;
she that vibrates, trembles, convulses,
and flies to sacred places.
She's the one who opens her breast
to shed grace from her heart;
and licks the tundra with her fire
elevating beyond desire
the sacred, secret art.
She evaporates reason
to shield you from the din,
and all the baseless treason.
Allow her to flay off your skin,
she'll give you birth anew;
A saint is one who knows the world
that matters, that is true.

Thank You Note

By Zenith Candlebaum

Thank you for deliverance
from the festering wound.
Despair almost consumed
this blessed, precious chance.

Once again I am open
to life's sweet mystery,
and veiled as it may be
hope has been reawoken.

Thank you for sanctuary,
the tempest has been quelled.
My will is now propelled
towards prosperity.

The enemies I've conquered,
the monsters from within,
now I can call my kin
so peace has been conferred.

Thank you for love and passion

for seeing into my heart;
the withered, empty tart
is now filled with compassion.

Beauty flutters again
surprising all my senses.
Darkness is just past tenses.
Pure light has filled this glen.

•••

Unwelcome she comes
taking both flower and fruit;
life cracks, upended.

Blind Side of The Sun

By Zenith Candlebaum

As I lay down beside you
Soft dirt around my skin
I wonder where you're going
Desperate for where you've been

The wood she speaks in whispers
Dividing us in two
Forever lost your piercing stares
I'm so far away from you

I can still hear you breathing
When I lay in my bed
My mornings seem so fleeting
As dreams muddle my head

Caught in this blazing winter
Your eyes the purest white
My nails, they scratch the wood unfair
Aching to get inside

Why do you have to sleep away

In another place, where all are one?
And if you're gone, why should I stay
On the blind side of the sun?

I miss you...

Turning The Page

To build a tower for the ages
and tear it down within a day
seemed at first the only lesson
that Zenith had to master.

But life with her had shown him stages,
and so joy came without delay
to break open the hindering prison
where grief becomes disaster.

When she set sail, first there were rages,
he wanted life itself to slay;
then came the calm, and intuition
spread open the last chapter.

The search is hidden within pages
of books that morph what they portray;
everyone is a progression
forever growing vaster.

And therein lies the final lesson:
beyond singular love,
divine intention.

Dragon

The warrior-monk was sitting on a rock
engaged in conversation with a fish.
Zenith chuckled at the sight when he heard the carp's
reply:
"Why do you come to me with such conundrums?
I'm nothing but a fish swimming upstream."

A million times he'd lived that scene
with fish and birds, with trees and mentors,
looking for the answer to the sum of all his questions;
that endless merry-go-round flooding his head.

He had come to the Order hoping to find peace and
wisdom.
There, nestled in the forest, tempered by the mountain
winds
he had found that and more.

He'd understood that words and reason
could only go so far,
and so, asking the question was
a self-fulfilling trap.

Demanding concrete answers got him stuck in

limitations,
the tangled web of stories that arranges human life;
a consensual fiction,
moving, beautiful, and joyful,
but nevertheless, a prison.

He had come to the conclusion that freedom requires no
story,
which does not give you leave to depart before your
time.
Instead, it means becoming every story ever told,
 just as the ones unfolding, and those that are still to
come.

He'd learned that every path has in it all the answers
planted,
and at the monastery, he had watched the seedlings
grow.
Having witnessed his own, he now recognized in others
the answers that revealed parts of the whole.

The fish was right:

You are what you are at every moment,
but never a single thing;
in constant transformation,

always living, dying, changing,
always swimming upstream.